CREEPY CRAWLIES

Illustrated by Peter Scott

Written by Sarah Khan

Designed by Reuben Barrance

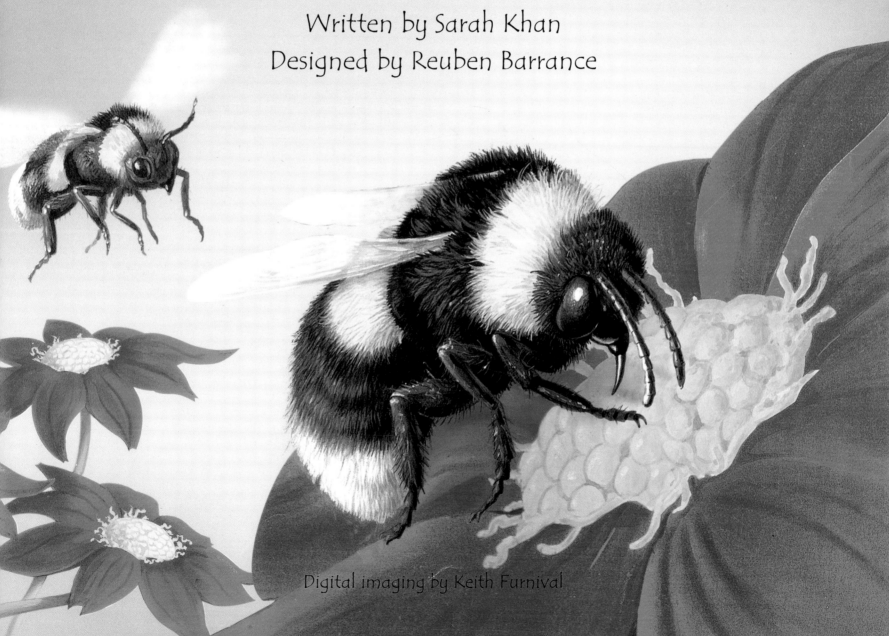

Digital imaging by Keith Furnival

Spiders and flies

Spiders spin webs using sticky
threads they make in their bodies.
They weave their webs to catch flies.

Lift the flaps
to see a spider
spinning her web.

Flies and other insects are trapped by the sticky threads of the web.

The spider can feel the web trembling.

Slugs and snails

Slugs and snails like to live where it's damp and cool.

This is a slug. Slugs and snails make slippery slime to help them glide along.

It's a long way down...

Who has made this shiny trail?

This is a snail. Snails love to munch on leaves.

They scrape off pieces of leaf with their rough, raspy tongues.

In hot weather, snails stay in their shells to stop them from drying out.

Where's my mum?

Bees and wasps

Bees and wasps flap their wings very quickly when they fly. This makes a buzzing sound.

This is a bumble bee. Its body is big and furry.

Phew! I'm glad bees don't eat maggots!

Wasps love to eat very ripe fruit. Which of these plums will a wasp like the most?

Wasps look different from bees. They aren't as furry and have brighter stripes.

Oh dear! I hope that wasp doesn't see me.

Caterpillars and butterflies

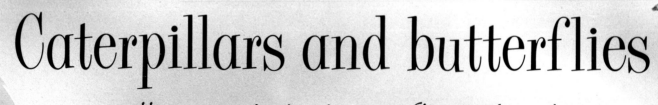

Caterpillars are baby butterflies. They look very different from grown-up butterflies. They change shape and colour as they grow.

The little caterpillar has just crawled out of a tiny, green egg.

I'm so hungry!

First, the caterpillar eats the egg. Then, it starts to munch on leaves.

When the caterpillar is fully grown, it stops eating and takes a long, long rest.

Now I'm full up.

It makes a case around itself and starts to turn into a butterfly.

Ants

Ants live together in big groups called colonies. They work in teams to find food.

These ants are going out to look for food.

This is a desert seed pod. There are tasty seeds inside it.

Ladybirds

It's good to have ladybirds in your garden because they eat greenflies. Greenflies suck the juice from flowers and make them dry up.

A ladybird can eat over 50 greenflies in one day.

What a juicy rosebud!

When a ladybird flies, ~~she lifts her~~ ...ases...

This ladybird has laid her eggs on the underside of a leaf. In a few days, the babies will hatch out.

Different types of ladybird have a different number of spots on their bodies.

I've got lots of spots. Where are yours?

I don't have any at all.

Fireflies

Fireflies aren't really flies at all. They are a kind of beetle.

When evening comes, you can see their bodies glowing in the dark.

Where are you?

Male fireflies flash their lights on and off to make the females look at them.

Crickets

Here's a hungry cricket. She eats lots of things, but she doesn't eat fireflies.

I don't eat flashy food!

The firefly's light warns her that he will taste bad.

CHIRP! CHIRP! CHIRP! CHIRP! CHIRP!

Who's making that chirping sound?

This book has shown you just some of the millions of tiny creatures that creep and crawl through gardens, fields and deserts all over the world. But it would take many thousands of books like this to show them all...

Edited by Kirsteen Rogers
Cover design by Karen Tomlins

First published in 2004 by Usborne Publishing Ltd, Usborne House,
83-85 Saffron Hill, London EC1N 8RT, England.
www.usborne.com
Copyright © Usborne Publishing Ltd, 2004.

Printed in China.